St Helier Town Hall.

Dr Caspar, Baron von Aufsess's predecessor at the Feldkommandantur, Jersey, riding his horse, Satan, near Mont Orgeuil.

Translation of a Communication addressed to the Governor of the Isle of Jersey.

1st July, 1940.

To the Chief of the Military and Civil Authorities

Jersey (St. Helier).

1. I intend to neutralize military establishments in Jersey by occupation.

2. As evidence that the Island will surrender the military and other establishments without resistance and without destroying them, a large White Cross is to be shown as follows, from 7 a.m. July 2nd, 1940.
   a. In the centre of the Airport in the East of the Island.
   b. On the highest point of the fortifications of the port.
   c. On the square to the North of the Inner Basin of the Harbour.

   Moreover all fortifications, buildings, establishments and houses are to show the White Flag.

3. If these signs of peaceful surrender are not observed by 7 a.m. July 2nd, heavy bombardment will take place.
   a. Against all military objects.
   b. Against all establishments and objects useful for defence.

4. The signs of surrender must remain up to the time of the occupation of the Island by German troops.

5. Representatives of the Authorities must stay at the Airport until the occupation.

6. All Radio traffic and other communications with Authorities outside the Island will be considered hostile actions and will be followed by bombardment.

7. Every hostile action against my representatives will be followed by bombardment.

8. In case of peaceful surrender, the lives, property, and liberty of peaceful inhabitants are solemnly guaranteed.

The Commander of the German Air Forces in Normandie,

——————————— **General**

The States have ordered this Communication to be printed and posted forthwith, and charge the Inhabitants to keep calm, to comply with the requirements of the Communication and to offer no resistance whatsoever to the occupation of the Island.

HITLER'S
FORTRESS
ISLANDS

Carel Toms

NEW ENGLISH LIBRARY
TIMES MIRROR

HITLER'S
FORTRESS
ISLANDS

© Carol Toms, 1967

First published in Great Britain by The New English Library
Limited in March, 1967
Re-issued in this new edition April 1971

NEL Books are published by The New English Library
Limited, from Barnard's Inn, Holborn, London, E.C.1.

Printed Offset Litho in Great Britain by
Cox & Wyman Ltd., London, Fakenham and Reading

45000 821 5

The author is grateful to numerous individuals as well as public and private bodies who assisted him in locating photographs, suggesting sources or supplying information for this book.

Principal sources of material came from collections held by La Société Jersiaise; Lord Coutanche, Jersey; the Royal Court Library, Guernsey; Priaulx Library, Guernsey; Guille-Allès Library, Guernsey; The Alderney Library; La Dame de Sark.

Other photographs and material were obtained from the Imperial War Museum; files of the Jersey *Evening Post;* archives of the Guernsey *Evening Press;* Jersey Underground Hospital; Guernsey Underground Hospital; Richard Heaume Collection; Baron von Aufsess; Reginald Blanchford; Mrs W. V. Drawmer; Mr and Mrs R. M. Thomason; Mr R. O. Falla; Mr A. K. Jory and Mr A. E. Gould.

Sources consulted were: *Islands in Danger* (Wood); *Jersey Diary, The German Occupation of Jersey* (Sinel); *Guernsey under German Rule* (Durand); *Jersey under the Jackboot* (Maugham); *Isolated Island* (Cortvriend); *Jersey under the Swastika* (Mollet); *Samaritan of the Islands* (Everitt); *Five Years of German Occupation* (Leale); *Hitler Invaded Sark* (Marshall); *The Dame of Sark* (Sibyl Hathaway); *Herm, Its Mysteries and Charm* (Marshall); *Stamps of the Channel Islands* (Baker); *The German Occupation of Jersey* (La Société Jersiaise); *Inside Hitler's Headquarters* (Warlimont) and other works of reference.

CONTENTS

A sergeant and ten soldiers took over Sark at the beginning of the occupation. At the end there were almost three hundred. This picture shows German troops marching along the Avenue.

It is strictly forbidden to take photographs at the airports without a permit from the airport commandant.

THE LEGACY

Hitler's mark on the Channel Islands will never be obliterated. Under his direct orders an impregnable fortress was created which became nothing but a useless ploy. And this methodical and fanatical urge to build walls of steel and concrete round the islands may well go down in history as one of his greatest follies.

There were immense preparations against attack which never came and gigantic installations which were hardly used. There was a huge underground building programme which was never completed and a complicated coastal defence system against every possible form of invasion which was never seriously attacked.

For all the sweated labour which brought despair and death to the forced labourers and for all the fire power so cunningly devised, the islands were regained by British forces in 1945 almost as simply as they were taken by German forces in 1940.

Today there is little to see of these defence works. All that was destructible has been destroyed. But the islands are still left with a legacy of phantom-like holes in the earth; smelly bunkers, gaunt towers, weed-grown gun emplacements, machine-gun positions and searchlight batteries.

Islanders ignore these reminders of five years of terror, suppression and near starvation and it is only the visitor who asks questions about these mouldering chambers, built with great speed, which now stand as memorials to a vast international brigade of workers who were trapped in the Hitlerite war machine and forced to work or starve.

An observation post at La Moye, Jersey.

The occupation story has been told by a succession of authors, the best known work being that of the late Alan and Mary Wood, whose book, *Islands in Danger*, is considered the standard work on the period and is published as a Four Square paperback.

Hitler's Fortress Islands brings together the best of a vast collection of photographs drawn from numerous sources and presented to the reader as a documentary companion to *Islands in Danger*.

When the torch of freedom blazed again after the islands' total isolation from the outside world and the barbed wire was torn down for ever, the bleakness of half a decade gave way to new hopes for the future. Islanders wanted only to forget; but the grim grey years and the futility of it all seemed even more acute as they gazed in wonder at the war machine that successive waves of *Wehrmacht* had left behind.

In the wake of the dark invader were empty shops and empty stomachs and the islands were almost sinking under the weight of steel. Because of the memories it dredged up, islanders hated the sight of anything German. After the liberation, what then seemed the most unlikely objects for preservation are now collected as prize possessions.

Among these are photographs, many of which are printed here for the first time. This is a pictorial record taken from official German sources, private collections, public libraries and museums.

The Germans more than any other nation now realize the war was fought to liberate themselves as well as the rest of the world from the Nazi tyranny most of them once condoned. The Iron Curtain which still divides Germany is something the Germans in the West are able to see and touch and is a constant reminder to them that the frontiers of freedom end at notices which say "Stop. Danger. Soviet mines".

In West Germany today it is incredibly hard to believe that this nation was ever capable of any of the beastliness which history has marked

down against it. If it has learned a lesson, then perhaps the war was worth the sacrifice. This postscript in pictures concerns the only part of the British Empire ever to become occupied by the Germans during World War II and is intended also to serve as a constant reminder of the folly of war and the sweetness of freedom.

Only those Channel Islanders who suffered defeat, humiliation and suffering for almost five years will know the true meaning of being free.

Sketch map of the Channel Islands which appeared in Baron von Aufsess's book, 'Ein Bilderbogen von den Kanalinseln'.

PRELUDE TO OCCUPATION

In both islands women and children were given the chance of being voluntarily evacuated. They followed the schoolchildren.

People flocked to the ships on bicycles and in tomato lorries with suitcases filled to bursting point. Everyone who could make up his mind was in a hurry to get out.

With devastating suddenness the blitzkrieg swept through France like a forest fire. The march of events was quicker than one could think: it was only a matter of waiting helplessly until it happened.

By the middle of June, 1940, Channel Islanders were engulfed in a wave of unprecedented panic, the effects of which few people escaped. Earlier, the usual precautions had been taken: trenches had been dug, machine-gun posts manned and air-raid precautions observed. Then France fell before the Nazi onslaught and the occupation of the islands by German forces was seen to be inevitable. But no one knew for certain quite what to expect as a result of the German victory in France and up till 15 June, British troops were still landing in Jersey with their stores. But on 19 June the British Government finally ordered the total demilitarization of the islands.

On 21 June, the evacuation of children and men of military age was completed and the general public was fleeing to the evacuation ships as the States of Guernsey decided to form a Controlling Committee of eight men to run the island's affairs during the emergency. Bailiff Victor Carey also took on the civil duties of Lieutenant-Governor. The King's Attorney-General, Ambrose Sherwill, became president of the new committee.

The States of Jersey met on 24 June to form a Superior Council composed of eight departments to run the island. Bailiff Alexander Coutanche also took the office of the Lieutenant-Governor and became president of the Council. At this meeting a message from the King addressed to the two bailiffs confirmed the "strategic withdrawal" of British armed forces from the islands.

But the world at large was kept ignorant of Britain's withdrawal and after a further three days of suspense and gloomy foreboding came the terrifying and unexpected *Luftwaffe* bombardment of both islands.

Men of military age were then called upon to leave the islands and hundreds went immediately.

Jersey's famous West Park Pavilion, sandbagged and ready to take casualties, in August 1940.

St Peter Port's White Rock area was the 'Luftwaffe' target on the evening of 28 June 1940. Tomato lorries were bombed and many of their drivers killed. Bombs hit the clocktower at the weighbridge. St Helier received its share of the attacks and many buildings in and around the town were badly damaged or set on fire.

MESSAGE FROM THE KING TO THE
BAILIFFS OF JERSEY AND GUERNSEY

For strategic reasons it has been found
necessary to withdraw the Armed Forces
from the Channel Islands.

I deeply regret this necessity and I wish to
assure My people in the Islands that, in taking
this decision, My Government has not been
unmindful of their position. It is in their
interest that this step should be taken in
present circumstances.

The long association of the Islands with
the Crown and the loyal service the people of
the Islands have rendered to my ancestors
and Myself are guarantees that the link
between us will remain unbroken and I know
that My people in the Islands will look
forward with the same confidence as I do to
the day when the resolute fortitude with which
we face our present difficulties will reap the
reward of Victory.

On 28 June, German aircraft bombed and machine-gunned St Peter Port and St Helier. Twenty-nine people lost their lives in Guernsey and nine in Jersey. The St Peter Port lifeboat was shot up on her way to Jersey and the coxswain was killed.

The raiders flew over various parts of the islands dropping bombs here and there and spraying machine-gun bullets on defenceless islanders. Guernsey received the brunt of the attack: a line of tomato lorries—thought by *Luftwaffe* pilots to be ammunition trucks—was shot up and many of their drivers killed outright.

An ambulance was also machine-gunned. One Lewis gun on board the steamer *Isle of Sark* in St Peter Port which was about to take away one of the last boatloads of evacuees, was the only means of defence left in the island.

In Jersey bombs were dropped at La Rocque and in the vicinity of St Helier harbour. Houses were damaged at South Hill and stores were set ablaze in Commercial Buildings.

Message from the King which was read by the bailiffs of both islands to their respective States' assemblies, but which was never published in the newspapers.

An unauthorized poster which had a certain calming effect on the population of Guernsey during the height of the evacuation crisis period. About 10,000 of Jersey's 51,000 population left and 20,000 of Guernsey's population of nearly 44,000 evacuated.

St Peter Port's White Rock area was the 'Luftwaffe' target on the evening of 28 June 1940. Tomato lorries were bombed and many of their drivers killed. Bombs hit the clocktower at the weighbridge. St Helier received its share of the attacks and many buildings in and around the town were badly damaged or set on fire.

VISITORS
IN GREY

The *Luftwaffe* had the honour of taking the Channel Islands. It was a simple, swift operation carried out without a shot being fired. Islanders and members of the States were ready to receive the enemy.

Guernsey was occupied on the evening of Sunday, 30 June, but few people were aware it had passed into German hands until they received their newspapers free next day with the orders of the first Commandant.

Pouches cut from bed linen belonging to the captain of a French air-force squadron, whose deserted headquarters in Normandy had been taken over by the *Luftwaffe*, were hurriedly sewn together and into each of three of such home-made devices was sewn a small bag into which sand ballast was placed. Each pouch contained a signed ultimatum which was rolled into a cardboard cylinder. According to a German account of the operation quoted in *Jersey under the Jackboot*, Lieutenant Kern was the man selected to fly alone over the islands, delivering surrender summonses from the air.

Three were dropped in Jersey, one of which landed on the spiked railings of a St Helier church. It was made of red and blue ribbon, was several yards long and tapered into "tails" which fluttered like streamers as it plunged to the ground.

In Guernsey a German plane landed at the airport, took off in a hurry when chased by RAF planes and landed again. Only a police inspector and three police officers were aware of the invaders' presence. A party of German officers was driven to the Royal Hotel and Bailiff Victor Carey and His Majesty's Attorney-General Ambrose Sherwill were summoned.

The early days of 1940 were times of victory songs, marching bands, the tramp of jackboots and a silent population. Troops marched or rode in commandeered cars and other vehicles.

German forces made a mad rush for the well-stocked shops in both islands during the early days of the occupation.. Troops paid in 'Reichkredit-kassen' notes—Occupation Marks—which came in useful when official Channel Islands buying commissions went to France to purchase vital supplies.

In 1940 it was soon evident there would be a shortage of domestic fuel and many tons of peat were dug at St Ouen's Bay, Jersey, and from a bog at Vazon, Guernsey.

This is what Guernsey looked like to Lieutenant Kern of the 'Luftwaffe' as he flew over the island just before he dropped in at the airport on 30 June 1940.

News from England

For the Channel Islands

No. 2 SEPTEMBER 30, 1940   DISTRIBUTED BY THE R.A.F.

GERMAN FRONT LINE BATTERED

Dover, September 24.

WATCHERS on this coastline will never forget the skies of moving light and fire which they have seen night after night in recent weeks enveloping, like an Aurora Borealis of the south, the ports where the Germans are massed for their attempted invasion.

With members regularity the R.A.F. have destroyed the enemy barges, their stores, barracks, fuel and ammunition dumps.

BOMBS FOR BERLIN

STRANGLEHOLD BY THE NAVY

American View

"—YOU'RE TELLING ME!"

LEAVES AND NEWS

AUTUMN leaves are falling as well as war copies of News from England. They may seem a gloomy enough reminder that the summer is over and a second bad winter is setting in—this one under the alien hand of fortune.

ESCAPE FROM GUERNSEY

Eight Reach Britain

London, September 11

A PARTY of eight men have successfully escaped from Guernsey to England in a 20 ft. boat. The London press is headlining their adventures.

They left Guernsey under cover

A few days later another NEWS FROM ENG-
LAND leaflet raid took place. Whenever leaflets
were dropped, German soldiers were detailed to
scour the countryside for them. They were also
forbidden to read them. Islanders were told it was
their duty to hand them over to the Field Commandant.

BEKANNTMACHUNG.

Im Monat Juli wurden auf der Insel Guernsey 2 englische Offiziere zu Erkundungswecken an Land gesetzt. Die beiden Offiziere hielten sich zeitweilig bei ihren Angehoerigen auf, ohne die deutsche Militaerbehoerde von ihrem Aufenthalt ordnungsgemaess in Kenntnis zu setzen.

Die Namen der betr. Angehoerigen sind:

Frau Adele Masurier, geb. Martel, wohnhaft West-Craft, Queen's Road, St. Peter-Port und

Frau Dorothy Madeleine Michael, geb. Moorhouse, Le Paradou, Forest.

Um in Zukunft jede Unterstuetzung seitens der Zivilbevoelkerung von weiteren britischen Spaehversuchen auf den besetzten Kanalinseln zu unterbinden, wurde vom zustaendigen Armeeoberkommando angeordnet, dass die beiden Frauen nach einem auf dem Festlande gelegenen, mindestens 15 km von der Kueste entfernten Platz gebracht werden und sich dort taeglich bei der Feldkommandantur zu melden haben.

Feldkommandantur 515.
Der Feldkommandant
gez. Schumacher
Oberst.

NOTICE.

During July two British officers landed on the Island of Guernsey for the purpose of gathering military information. Temporarily, they put up with relatives without informing the German military authorities of their stay according to regulations.

The relatives are:

Mrs. Adele Masurier, née Martel, Westcraft, Queen's Road, St. Peter Port, and

Mrs. Dorothy Madeleine Michael, née Moorhouse, Le Paradou-Forest.

To prevent the civil population of the Channel Islands from supporting henceforth British Agents on occupied territory, the Commander in Chief of the Army ordered the two ladies to be removed to a place on the Continent, at least 9 miles distant from the coast, where they will have to present themselves daily before the local Feldkommandant.

Feldkommandantur 515.
Der Feldkommandant.
(Signed) Schumacher, Colonel.

The public notice which says that Mrs Adele
Masurier and Mrs Dorothy Madeleine Michael
are to be removed to the Continent because two
British officers "put up with relatives without
informing the German military authorities of their
stay".

St Helier Town Hall was taken over on 2 July as the Commandant's headquarters. There was a guard constantly on duty at the main door.

Next day in Jersey Bailiff Alexander Coutanche read the ultimatum to a large crowd
in the Royal Square. Late in the afternoon he
drove to the airport with several States
officials to meet the invaders.

The terms of unconditional surrender were
complied with in both islands. Captain
Gussek became first Commandant in Jersey,
where he set up office at the Town Hall on
2 July. The same day, Dr Albrecht Lanz
arrived in Guernsey, to take over there as
Commandant.

Everything was peaceful and sweet reason-
ableness prevailed. Cricket matches continued
to be played. Football matches were arranged
between islanders and Germans. Swimming
galas took place. There were trips to Sark and
an inter-island mail and passenger service
recommenced.

The troops were in paradise. The weather was
perfect and the islands looked their best.
The beaches were empty and the shops were
full. The "visitors" bought as much as they
wanted for themselves and to send home.
They commandeered, placarded, paraded,
marched, sang victory songs and held band
concerts. They were going to be in England
before the end of August.

But small clouds were already gathering on
the otherwise sunny Nazi horizon. While the
islands' authorities were complying with
every new German regulation and demand,
during the first week of the occupation, a
Guernsey-born lieutenant in The Royal
Hampshires landed from a British submarine
at dead of night on the south coast of
Guernsey. He was Hubert Nicolle whose
mission was to gather information about
enemy defences.

When he left the island on the third evening,
two more officers were landed: Lieutenant
Philip Martel of The Hampshires and
Lieutenant Desmond Mullholland of the
Duke of Cornwall Light Infantry. Their job
was to spy the land in preparation for a
commando raid.

The DAILY MIRROR reproduced the 1 July edition of THE STAR, in which the Orders of Commandant were given front-page treatment. The story was told to a MIRROR reporter by a group of Guernseymen who escaped from the island the day after the Germans landed.

The operation misfired. Mullholland and Martel—in civilian clothes—failed to get away and after obtaining British uniforms finally surrendered and were made prisoners of war. During their visit they contacted their nearest relatives, Mrs A. E. Le Masurier and Mrs A. C. Martel. Both women were arrested and charged with harbouring the fugitives. They were jailed at St Lo for six months.

Unknown to Martel and Mullholland, Operation Ambassador—the first commando raid of the war—took place under Lieutenant-Colonel John Durnford Slater, who described it later as "almost a comic failure". Landing was made at Jerbourg, Guernsey and on the night of 13-14 July the only thing achieved amounted to rolling stones from a garden rockery into the road near the Doyle Column at Jerbourg. The incident was described by the Germans as "a grave act of sabotage".

Another matter which started an early deterioration in relations between islanders and occupiers occurred when eight men escaped in a boat from Bordeaux on 6 September 1940. But a far more serious event which ended in fifteen people being sent to prison in France was after Hubert Nicolle had again landed on the island.

On 4 September he arrived with Lieutenant Jim Symes, another islander. The families and friends of these two British agents were all accused of harbouring them while they made unsuccessful attempts to escape. After they had surrendered on 21 October, Mr Sherwill himself was arrested, deprived of his dual position as president of the Controlling Committee and that of Attorney-General and sent to a jail in Paris. The two officers were sent to prisoner-of-war camps.

Sherwill's post as Controlling Committee president was taken over by John Leale, who

HITLER'S "JERSEY LILIES"

SCORES of Hitler Youth girls, mostly dressed in white blouses and shorts, have arrived in Jersey on a "cultural mission."

The towns and villages are full of them, though how the inhabitants will react to their "culture" is not yet apparent, especially as the Islanders are allowed only two meals a day—poor meals at that.

And "culture," especially of the Nazi model—girls or no girls —needs something to swallow with it.

Most of Jersey's produce is being sent to France to replace French crops seized by Germany, and the invaders are doing nothing to alleviate the growing food shortage.

Private stocks of food and wines

told the States after the war that the Germans threatened—unless they were satisfied no one was harbouring members of the British Army—to shoot twenty of the leading citizens. The Germans instituted collective reprisals because of the Nicolle-Symes affair and ordered the confiscation of all wireless sets in the Bailiwick. Nearly 13,000 sets were collected. On Christmas Eve, when the Germans announced that those sent to prison in connection with the affair were to be released, the radio sets were given back. It was Christmas "as usual".

Hitler's "Jersey Lilies". From the SUNDAY EXPRESS, 3 November 1940.

The Guernsey airport building, pock-marked by raiding RAF aircraft, sandbagged and flying the Nazi flag, was the first building entered by the Germans when they landed in the Channel Islands on 30 June 1940.

SENTENCED TO DEATH

On 17 March 1941, the Rev. Père Maré, a Catholic priest of Jersey received a message from the Germans to the effect that a member of his religion required the Last Rites.

At six o'clock that morning he went to the Grand Hotel. There he was told by the Germans that François Marie Scornet, a twenty-one-year-old French patriot had been sentenced to death and was to be shot "because of his favouring the actions of the enemy by wilfully supporting England in the war against the German Empire".

Scornet's crime was that he led a band of French boys who escaped from Brittany in January 1941, with the intention of sailing to England. They landed on the west coast of Guernsey, mistaking the island for the Isle of Wight and were captured and taken to Jersey. Their trial took place in the Old Committee Room of Jersey's Royal Court and Scornet, who took full responsibility, faced the firing squad at St Ouen's Manor, where a memorial stone is to be seen today.

Père Maré was permitted to stay with the condemned youth for the last two hours of his

Memorial stone to François Marie Scornet, at St Ouen's Manor, Jersey, near the spot where he was executed.

François Marie Scornet, shot by a German firing squad at St Ouen's Manor, Jersey, on 17 March 1941.

life. He went to St Ouen's Manor where Scornet was already pinioned to an oak tree. The priest embraced the youth, gave him his crucifix to kiss and Scornet's last words were "Long live God! Long live France!"

Scornet's companions—fifteen in all—were imprisoned and four of them died. Another, Jacques Poisson, escaped and was later killed fighting with the Maquis.

Posters such as this were continually being put up as a grave warning to the population. This Frenchman, Robert Deregnaucourt, a chauffeur of Paris, was condemned to be shot on 10 January 1941, by a German court martial for "acts of violence".

NOTICE:

LOUIS BERRIER,

a resident of Ernes
is charged with having
released a pigeon with
a message for England.
He was, therefore, sentenced

TO DEATH

for espionage by the
Court Martial and

SHOT

on the 2nd of August.

August 3rd, 1941.   Court Martial

OPERATION TRANSPORT

STATES OFFICE.

GUERNSEY.

23rd Oct 1940.

Dear Sir/or Madam,—

I beg to inform you that your Motor Vehicle, Registered No. _1725_ has been acquired by the German Authorities for the price of _25,800_ Francs. = £147-10-0.

I hold the receipt for the vehicle and the acknowledgement of the purchase price, settlement for which will be made by me in due course.

In the meantime please complete the enclosed form of declaration, and return it to me, together with the registration book relating to the vehicle.

Yours faithfully,

H. Champ...

States Supervisor.

a.a. Gould
Rochdale
Ville au Roi

When the Germans first arrived in the islands they commandeered cars without authority and used as much petrol as they could get hold of. But in less than three months Operation Transport was organized— from their point of view.

Requisition orders went out and car owners received notification to deliver their vehicles at stated depots, with a note of the price they required. A few days later the owner would receive a polite note to the effect that his vehicle had been acquired by the German authorities.

Vehicle number 1925 has been acquired by the German authorities for the price of 25,800 Francs (£147 10s).

As military installations grew, so did the number of signs directing German forces to them. Every road was thoroughly signposted and labelled. This picture shows the Guernsey press censor in his car near the Royal Hotel.

Cars commandeered by the German authorities on the Albert Pier, St Peter Port.

This horse-drawn ambulance, used in Guernsey, was specially constructed from hundred-year-old plans. A pair of German Army horses were used to draw it, but owing to the fodder shortage, its use was limited and it was only employed for non-urgent cases. This vehicle was later used in Sark, when it was towed by a tractor.

Guernsey police officer and a German chauffeur
and by the Commandant's car while he pays a
sit to the Little Chapel and grotto at Les
auxbelets.

The number of cars hidden in haystacks and other strange places is not known but some islanders were not slow to devise ways and means of beating the Germans at every game. It was, indeed, surprising how many pre-1939 cars suddenly appeared on the roads in 1945!

Driving on the left of the road was instituted from the beginning of the Occupation. Then other orders started to creep in and international road signs were introduced in 1942. This was a sensible enough move because although most islanders were deprived of their motor vehicles, they had to get from place to place and they also had to share the roads with German drivers who often drove at dangerous speeds. Many of the roads were improved at dangerous corners and junctions to take the extremely large vehicles and heavy traffic.

High-ranking German officers travelled in

Islanders soon grew accustomed to being issued with permits to do almost anything or to obtain almost any commodity. This is a special driving licence for the driver of a van.

ZULASSUNGS - BESCHEINIGUNG.
DRIVING LICENCE.

Listen Nr. 119
(No)

Der-Die   V an (1935) 12 HP. Pol. Kennzeichen 1198
         (Fahrzeuggattung)   (Reg. No.)
         (Description Class of Vehicle)

Motornummer 146046   Fahrgestell Nr. H 5372
(Engine No.)   (Chassis No.)

Anschrift des Eigentumers   H. J. Baal,
(Name and Address of owner)
                    11 Cheapside.

ist zur Weiterbenutzung bis zum (from) 31 OCT. 1940 zugelassen.
(Is Licensed)

                am (to)   SEP. 1940

Der Fahrer des Fahrzeuges ist   D. Gallichan
(The driver of the Vehicle is)

2 Henley Cottages Spurnprove Personalausweis Nr.
                        oder Fahrerschein Nr.
                        (Personal Permit or Driving Licence No.)

Stempel des   den   9 SEP. 1940
Feldkommandantur   (Date)

                    J. ...
                    (President Department Transport and Communication.)

chauffeur-driven commandeered cars or went on horseback, while islanders were forced to use horse-drawn transport, bicycles or their feet. The variety of vehicles seen on the roads included tanks, tracked vehicles, lorries, armoured trucks, huge trailers and steam trains.

It was not an unusual occurrence to see abandoned cars with a breakdown notice stating that the vehicle was in need of repair.

Horse buses were used from the beginning of the Occupation. They were converted from vans once used to cart potatoes or tomatoes to the harbours.

A high-ranking German officer pays a visit to
Brelade's Cemetery, Jersey, which was used as
place of interment for all German forces who di
in the island.

A German tank rumbles along a country lane, followed by an islander on a bicycle.

Narrow gauge railway tracks were laid in Jersey and Guernsey and several steam locomotives were brought over from France to operate the "services". Their use was designed to save petrol and they transported many millions of tons of cement, sand, granite, steel and other materials used in the building of defences. This one ran along the esplanade at St Peter Port. A favourite game played by Jersey children was placing stones on the railway lines.

On 15 July 1942, Leslie Sinel reported in his JERSEY DIARY that the Germans officially opened the railway which connected the piers with Millbrook. The Commandant blew a whistle and the engine, after a couple of attempts to get away, commenced its journey after a decorated tape had been cut. A band enlivened the proceedings and a commemorative dinner was held at the Pomme d'Or Hotel. The Germans declared that this was only the beginning. They intended to extend the railways which would be used by troops and civilians.

The bicycle was as good a mode of transport as any in the islands—even for the German Army—after the blitzkreig had come to a grinding halt.

One of the strangest sights in Guernsey was that of people queuing for a ration of sea water in which to boil vegetables when salt was unobtainable. Tankers were taken by lorry to certain depots where distribution took place.

On 20 October 1941, on Hitler's own initiative, he issued an OKW (Supreme Command) order for "the build-up and defence of the English Channel Islands". This instruction stated that "large-scale operations against the Western occupied areas remain unlikely", but it continued that "account must be taken of the possibility that the English may at any time carry out isolated attacks as the result of pressure from their Eastern allies and for political and propaganda reasons; in particular they may attempt to recapture the Channel Islands, which are of considerable importance for our escort traffic".

Walter Warlimont states in *Inside Hitler's Headquarters* that with the order, Hitler virtually transferred responsibility for the Western occupied areas from OKH (Army High Command) to OKW.

Orders for the fortification of the Channel Islands went into immense detail and went so far as to state the number and type of coastal batteries, details of reinforced concrete works and the thickness of their walls in millimetres. Monthly reports had to be rendered on the course of their construction and Hitler collected a mass of large-scale maps which he kept locked in his own desk.

He even ordered disciplinary punishment one day for the officer responsible for keeping these maps up to date because one anti-aircraft battery too many or too few had been shown in the islands.

Soon after the order was issued men and material started pouring into the islands. The harbours were jammed with shipping of all kinds: barges, floating cranes, trawlers, tugs, fast patrol boats and other craft. There was a continuous stream of sea traffic from the Continent to the islands which was occasionally interrupted by Allied air raids

In the north of Guernsey, Strong Point Le Marchant was designed to prevent Allied landing attempts. The French coastal guns could fire a 32 lb shell with 1,000 yards range. In support was a searchlight for which the Germans generated their own electricity.

but which brought millions of tons of material for the building of the "impregnable fortress". Guernsey and Alderney were in the front line of these defences and these islands were chosen for the siting of the largest guns, rather than Jersey, which was nearer the Continent. Preparations were now well in hand so that Allied invasion was "out of the question".

The defence of St Peter Port was rated high. In this sector the garrison was ordered to defend its strong point "to the last man", against any enemy attacking from the land, sea or air. The New Jetty was prepared for blowing up should the Allies have attacked. After Liberation, 207 27 cm shells were removed from the piles.

Hitler decreed that for the Army it was urgent to provide a close network of emplacements, as far as possible with flanking fire, which must be well concealed and have sufficient guns of the size required to pierce 100 mm. armour plate for defence against tanks which may be landed from flat-bottomed boats; accommodation for mobile diversion parties and armoured cars.

General Hans Speidel, Chief of Staff to Rommel, stated in his book, *Invasion*, that by the spring of 1944 there were 11 heavy batteries with 38 strong points ready to defend the 148 kilometres of coastline on the islands; whereas on the whole front, from Dieppe to St Nazaire—over 1,000 kilometres —there were the same number of batteries and 37 strong points.

The strength of the garrison on the islands was to be one whole division supported by an anti-aircraft regiment and a tank regiment. After the Allied landings in Normandy on 6 July 1944, Rommel made frantic appeals to have the 319 Division withdrawn from the islands, but he was told, "According to intelligence reports from higher authorities, an attack on the Channel Islands by 40 to 50 commando groups approximating to a division, is daily expected".

As the situation got worse, it soon became obvious that the Division would be trapped and when the war ended in May 1945, there were 35,000 men in the islands who had not struck a blow.

In a German tactical review dated 1 September 1944, the islands are mentioned in order of military importance: Guernsey, Jersey, Alderney. Each of the 11 battalions of the 319 Division was allocated 13 kilometres of coastline. The document stated that Jersey has large, sandy bays which "are now protected by armoured walls". In Guernsey the danger points were the larger bays of L'Ancresse, Grand Havre and Vazon, where there were possibilities of landings being made simultaneously for "one or two companies". Aptly describing Guernsey's physical outline,

Bastion North,
Castle Cornet, St Peter Port,
through the barbed wire.

A camouflaged casemate gun
in position at
Soldiers' Bay, Guernsey.

Low tide at the Old Harbour, St Peter Port.

Ringing the coasts, control towers such as this at La Corbière, Jersey, are still to be seen. The camouflage is made to represent granite masonry. Now used by the Jersey harbour authorities as a radio station.

the review says the surface is "like a roof with the south coast the gable". The population of Guernsey is given at 20,000, 40 per cent of whom are "in the ports". Jersey has a population of 40,000, with 50 per cent in the ports, the remainder being distributed over the whole island. The population of Alderney is given as nil.

If Hitler ever saw this document he might have realized some of the hazards with which German-controlled shipping had to contend. A note on "nautical and weather conditions" states that with an 8-metre rise and fall of tide at Guernsey and 10 metres at Jersey and 7 metres in Alderney, mine laying was a difficult matter. It was also noted that there were currents up to 8 knots and that the weather was "very changeable".

Conditions were particularly difficult in St Helier harbour where, up to the beginning of September 1944, there had been 10 shipping casualties—mostly total losses. Among these is noted the *Schockland* off Jersey with 130 dead (50 per cent).

Up to the start of the D-Day operation there had been 22 air raids on ships and ports in the islands in which 93 people were killed, 250 wounded and in which 12 ships had been sunk and 13 vessels damaged.

The principal air raids noted were in November 1941 on "General Vara" and "Captain Mirus", which almost certainly refer to gun batteries of that name. In January 1942, there was another raid on St Peter Port, in which the town received considerable damage from blast.

There was much action at sea during this period and eight naval battles are mentioned, five of which were between Alderney and Cherbourg. In these actions 210 men died and 61 were wounded. Included in this number were 150 men on board two vessels which were a total loss in February 1942. One "incident" particularly noted was a German torpedo boat which was accidentally fired upon by another German vessel with the loss of 7 dead, including Colonel Christiani, Divisional Commander Supply Troops 319.

A French gun at Les Landes, Jersey.

Shells in a store at La Moye, Jersey.

In January 1942, three RAF Beauforts carried out a low-level attack on shipping in St Peter Port. Two ships were sunk. Attempts at salvage were made on both vessels by Matthews' Sark Party.

The White Hart Hotel, a waterside pub at St Peter Port, was converted into a blockhouse and inside its grim concrete walls and behind its steel doors—which still exist below ground—was housed the means of blowing the harbour installations sky-high.

A machine-gun position at Strong Point Calais, overlooking Fermain Bay, Guernsey.

Anti-tank defences at St Aubin's Bay, Jersey, where a short piece of concrete walling was built.

One of the many ships used by the Germans transport war material to the islands which came grief on the treacherous north coast of Jersey.

A group of officers inspecting fortifications in the L'Ancresse area of Guernsey.

There is a bramble-covered slot in the hillside at St Saviour's, Guernsey, which is the entrance to one of the most amazing German gun batteries ever erected in the islands. There were four guns in the Mirus battery, each housing a 48-ton, 12-inch (305 millimetre) gun with a range of 37 miles.

These incredible fortresses overlooked the sea at Le Frie Bâton, but now nothing is left except empty underground chambers where the weeds grow in profusion and the words *Feind hört mit* (The enemy may hear) printed on the walls, become fainter.

Each gun, its housing and equipment, was like the inside of a pocket battleship. Here was a shell room where the 250 kilo (500 lb) shells were transported by overhead rails; ventilation equipment, engine room, fuel chamber, central heating equipment, washing and sanitary facilities and accommodation for gun crews. Armour-piercing shells of 850 lb were also used.

This battery called Mirus has now practically disappeared into the countryside. It has also sunk into obscurity in the minds of people who remembered its might after the island's liberation, when they were able to visit it. At one site a new bungalow stands near the edge of a huge circular concrete bowl, inside which the giant turret, camouflaged like a farmhouse, revolved on its roller path. Today, this is like an amphitheatre and below are yawning chasms where the loading chamber, engine room and control position, as well as other vital instruments for plotting and computing, were housed.

The means of destruction vanished long ago and there is now nothing left but this concrete shell with a few curling, rusty pipes, spidery electric conduits and cobwebs on the walls. Silence reigns where once artillerymen practised a symphony of war and sang hate songs like *Gegen England* as they marched through the narrow lanes.

With barrel lowered the position looks like a small farmhouse.

The four guns were in action on ten occasions and each fired a total of 60 shells, many of which landed on Lihou Island, half a mile off Guernsey's west coast. This certainly was not a very impressive record but let us now go back to the beginning.

On 15 April 1914, the Russian battleship *Imperator Alexandr Trety* (Emperor Alexander III), of 27,300 tons displacement, was launched at Nicolaieff and commissioned early in 1917. She belonged to the Black Sea Fleet and after the Russian Revolution this battleship was renamed *Volya* (liberty).

Gun position camouflaged as farmhouse.

Each cordite container weighed 80 kilos.

Comparison with man to give idea of size of bore.

Comparison with man to give idea of size of gun barrel.

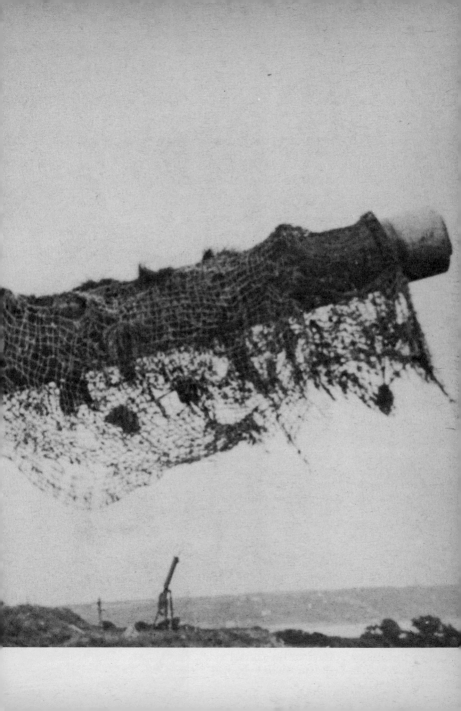

Early in 1918, after the German Crimean campaign, and in accordance with a German-Russian treaty, the *Volya* was placed at the disposal of the German Navy for police duties in the Black Sea after the collapse of Bulgaria and Turkey. The *Volya* was accordingly handed back by the Germans to the Russians. When Wrangel formed his White Army, all Russian warships of the Black Sea Fleet were incorporated in the White Navy. *Volya* became flagship and received the name *General Alexieff*. Finally she was transferred to Bizerta. She remained there until 1935 and was then broken up. As her guns were still usable they were stored at Bizerta naval dockyard.

In the winter of 1939-40, when the British and French Allied powers agreed to give material help to the Finns in their war against the Soviets, four of the twelve guns were loaded on board the steamer *Nina* for shipment via Norway to the north of Finland.

On the way, the ship's crew was surprised by the Norwegian campaign and the ship and guns were taken over by the Germans in a Norwegian harbour. They were then reconditioned by Krupp, supplied with mountings and shipped to Guernsey, where they were landed with a floating crane at St Julian's Pier.

Of the many islanders who recall seeing these guns being transported from St Peter Port to St Saviour's was Frank Le Page, a grocer, of St Martin's. He remembers standing in his shop at Ye Olde Forge Stores, when a customer warned him that a huge gun was being towed up the road on a trolley with twenty-four wheels.

Always eager to get a snapshot, Le Page had his camera with him and made a quick decision. It was early morning and had he tried to take his picture from inside the shop window—as he had taken so many before—the result would have been hopeless. So he dashed across the road to a friend's house, where the light was then on the correct side. From an upstairs bedroom window he had a

splendid view of one of these mighty gun barrels as it passed by. He took a couple of shots from the open window, but as he lowered his camera, a soldier guarding the rear of the vehicle, spotted him.

In this moment of crisis, Le Page shut the window, bolted downstairs, pushed the camera out of a window on to a roof which sloped steeply, and it rolled into a gutter. Expecting a knock on the front door, he dashed into the back garden, retrieved the camera from the gutter, crossed several back gardens to reach his own house and then took out the exposed film.

Putting in another film, he took a few shots of his house and garden. During the afternoon, the knock which he had expected came and Le Page was face to face with a German officer who demanded to know whether he had taken pictures of the gun.

He denied the charge and offered the camera to the unsuspecting officer who declined to take it, stating he would return next day. Fortunately for Le Page, he never came back, but the daring photographer had already decided to give up this kind of shooting for the rest of the war.

Preparing to transport a 500 lb shell on an overhead rail.

One of the four gun positions at Le Frie Bâton as it appears today.

Plan of one of the four Mirus batteries.

Frank Le Page's photograph of one of the Russian guns being transported to its position.

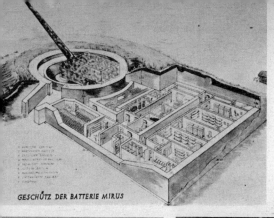

GESCHÜTZ DER BATTERIE MIRUS

Range clock and control instrument.

Control room.

Entrance to one of the underground bunkers.

PROPAGANDA

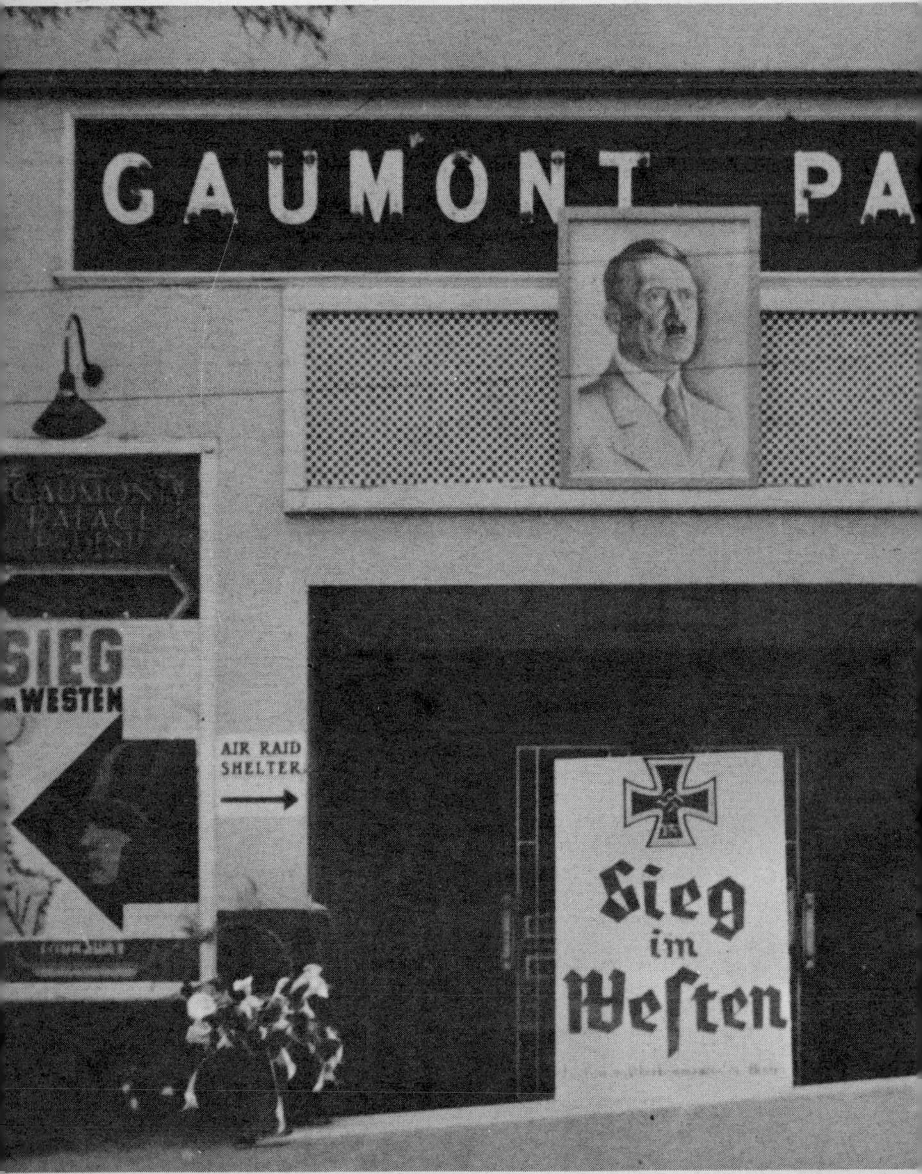

Nazi propaganda in the strictly censored and controlled press on both islands was countered by islanders who not only listened intently to BBC broadcasts but spread the news when radio receivers were banned.

The cinemas were soon taken over and propaganda films such as *Victory in the West* were shown both for the troops and for the islanders. Patrons were segregated, the stalls being reserved for civilians and the balcony for German troops only. Propaganda also extended to displays of books, photographs and posters in many shop windows and out of doors.

As early as 22 July 1940, on the order of the German authorities, the Jersey *Evening Post* was forced to publish a daily newspaper for the troops, *Deutsche Inselzeitung*. Jersey diarist Leslie Sinel wrote: "The Editor, Dr Kindt, said that this was the first German newspaper issued in the British Empire 'for the time being'; when reminded that though the island was well stocked, the winter was coming, he said there was no need to worry as the war would be over in three weeks, the subjugation of England being 'just a manoeuvre.'"

On the smaller island, Number One of the *Deutsche Guernsey Zeitung* printed by the Guernsey *Evening Press* was published on 4 July 1942, and contained a message from the Commander-in-Chief.

In June 1941, "V" for Victory signs started to appear on buildings and in public places throughout the islands. These signs, which islanders started to chalk up on walls or to paint in prominent places caused such a stir among the Germans that their first violent reaction was to threaten the confiscation of radio sets, fine the inhabitants and maintain a civilian guard to stop further actions of this kind.

'Victory in the West,' a film of the German High Command of the Army, was "presented" by the Gaumont Palace, Guernsey.

But the idea swept like wildfire throughout the islands and some people found making the signs were arrested and imprisoned. Suddenly the Germans started putting up "V" signs themselves and every house they occupied and every vehicle they used bore the familiar "V".

The German version of the "V" sign which appeared on most premises occupied by German troops throughout the Channel Islands.

In Guernsey, the troops did not have their own 'Deutsche Guernsey Zeitung' until 4 July 1942, when the first issue was printed.

NOTICE

FOR German films with English sub-titles the left-hand section of the stalls are reserved for <u>Civilians only</u>; the right-hand section and the Balcony for German troops only.

" La Gazette Officielle "

REWARD OF £25

A REWARD OF £25 WILL BE GIVEN TO THE PERSON WHO FIRST GIVES TO THE INSPECTOR OF POLICE INFORMATION LEADING TO THE CONVICTION OF ANYONE (NOT ALREADY DISCOVERED) FOR THE OFFENCE OF MARKING ON ANY GATE, WALL OR OTHER PLACE WHATSOEVER VISIBLE TO THE PUBLIC THE LETTER "V" OR ANY OTHER SIGN OR ANY WORD OR WORDS CALCULATED TO OFFEND THE GERMAN AUTHORITIES OR SOLDIERS.

THIS 8th·DAY OF JULY, 1941

VICTOR G. CAREY,

Bailiff.

Notice: Reward of £25.

Burton's window at the corner of King Street and Halkett Place, St Helier, was used to show off propaganda books, pamphlets, including 'The Decline and Fall of the British Empire'.

This German reaction came about after the Guernsey authorities had condemned the signs and a notice appeared in the newspapers offering a reward of £25 to anyone reporting information to the police which would lead to a conviction of persons responsible.

Neither warnings nor rewards stopped the incidents and a cartoon went the rounds depicting the unfortunate Bailiff Carey—who had signed the notice—in the role of Judas Iscariot hanging from a tree. When John Leale suggested to the Germans that they themselves adopted the signs as a means of stopping the practice, they did this in the islands, and throughout Europe there soon appeared German "V" signs on propaganda posters.

One Guernseywoman, Mrs Winifred Green, was sent to prison in Caen for four months for uttering the words "Heil Churchill" when she was a waitress at the Royal Hotel. At the German military court martial Mrs Green admitted saying a derogatory remark about Hitler and received her sentence.

After spending two weeks in the Guernsey jail she was marched to a boat at St Peter Port which was full of German soldiers. At Caen, Mrs Green found company in Kathleen Le Norman and Mrs Kinnaird—both from Jersey and imprisoned for making "V" signs. With nothing to do, Mrs Green borrowed a needle and tore a piece off her sheet and embroidered it with the pattern: Heil Churchill; RAF; Caen Prison, 1941. And of course, a "V" sign.

When she had served her sentence, Mrs Green sewed the embroidery in between the lining and cloth of her coat. She returned to Guernsey, went back to work at the Royal Hotel and became known as "Mrs Churchill".

Mrs Winifred Green, who was imprisoned for four months for saying "Heil Churchill".

The piece of sheet which Mrs Green embroidered in
a Caen prison and smuggled back to Guernsey

At the Forum, Jersey, the same film was being screened—'Sieg in Westen'.

There were no less than ten Jews in Jersey and Guernsey and all had to enter their names in a special register. Jewish-owned shops were placarded "Jewish Undertaking", and later Jewish businesses were ordered to be sold. Finally, all Jews in the islands were deported to Germany. Picture shows notice in Krichefski's shop in Halkett Street.

The Fifty Shilling Tailors in St Helier was also taken over as a bookshop.

IN HONOUR
OF THE DEAD

Channel Islanders were not slow to show their feelings when—as was so often to happen—bodies of Allied personnel were washed up on the shores of the islands. The military funerals which inevitably followed, to which the Germans paid due regard, gave islanders an opportunity to show their sympathy with those who suffered loss and their loyalty to Britain in a way which was among the most touching moments during the Occupation. In June 1943, the bodies of two RAF non-commissioned officers were washed ashore in Jersey. A military funeral was arranged and hundreds gathered along the route to Mont l'Abbe Cemetery. The coffins were each draped with a Union Jack and bore wreaths from the States of Jersey and the *Luftwaffe*. The German Air Force also provided bearers and a firing party. The bailiff laid two wreaths, one in the name of the King and the other on behalf of the States. Later, two lorry loads of wreaths were sent to the cemetery and hundreds of Jersey people filed past the graves.

In November 1943, the bodies of eighteen men from the Royal Navy were washed up on the shores of Guernsey and one in Sark. A further twenty-nine bodies were recovered in Jersey. A mass funeral for the men of *HMS Charybdis* and *HMS Limbourn* took place in each island on 17 November and those who attended will never forget the occasion.

Funeral service for the two RAF men in Jersey, which was attended by Bailiff Coutanche and other States officials.

This event was taken by islanders as an opportunity to show their loyalty and give thanks to the men fighting for their liberty. In Jersey the Germans seemed to be somewhat secretive about the funeral arrangements as though they feared a demonstration which might get out of control. Nevertheless hundreds of people attended and in Guernsey seven hundred wreaths were sent by islanders and there was no holding back their spontaneous feeling. Even the German Commandant

made an oration at the graveside, "We honour them as soldiers. They did their duty for their country."

Today, at St Luke's Cemetery, adjacent to the Howard Davis Park in Jersey, an inscription states, "This cemetery was dedicated on 26 November, 1943, as a resting place for the bodies of members of the Allied forces recovered within the Bailiwick during the Second World War." There are fifty-five graves.

GUERNSEY HONOURS FALLEN SAILORS

GUERNSEY pays tribute to British sailors who lost their lives when the cruiser Charybdis went down. Sixteen ratings were washed ashore on the island last November and were buried with full military honours. More than 7,000 wreaths were sent by the islanders, and 4,000 people were

The **DAILY MAIL** reproduced this picture of the funeral in Guernsey on 27 January 1944. The figures in the caption are inaccurate.

Mass funeral for twenty-nine of the forty-eight Royal Navy victims buried with full military honours at Le Foulon Cemetery, Guernsey.

TUNNEL UNDER THE CHURCH

The Germans tunnelled, bored and excavated a fantastic number of holes in Jersey and Guernsey in an effort to put vulnerable installations safely out of the way in the event of Allied attacks from the air. But the secrets of some of these tunnels may never be seen again. *Hohlgang* 12 *Munition* has been sealed up; nevertheless this grim memorial to German cunning will not be forgotten by those who watched it happen.

Long before the last chunk of granite was hewn from the underground tunnels below St Saviour's Church, in the heart of Guernsey, liberation came to the beleagured islands. It is estimated that eighteen thousand Organization Todt workers had arrived in Jersey and Guernsey by the start of 1942. They came from all over Europe and many were Russians. Their job was to work like slaves to convert the islands as quickly as possible into fortress outposts of the German Empire.

The work of excavating these underground hideouts for men, food and munitions, was done by this half-starved army of pathetic men clad in rags who endured lives of utter misery. They were locked in huts or old empty houses at night and driven to work before dawn each day by their khaki-clad OT officers who were in charge of the labour commandos.

For identification purposes, OT guards wore metal breast-plates.

Looking out of the main entrance, St Saviour's tunnel, Guernsey.

Organization Todt workers of the type employed to hew tunnels in the islands.

St Saviour's Church today
showing one of the now
overgrown tunnel entrances.

How many lives were lost in this and other similar gigantic undertakings, no one will know. The sweat, blood and toil put in by these men was prodigious. They burrowed and blasted for months on end and ton by laborious ton, the stone—pushed in trucks up and down small-gauge railway lines from inside the hill—was wheeled out and the rubble tipped into the valley.

In this green vale known as Sous l'Eglise (under the church) there is now only a faint suggestion that something had happened. The men with the whiplashes are gone and now there is only a hint of past activity. The pine trees have clothed the scarred hillside and nature has taken on the job of camouflaging the tracks along which men—with their backs bent in toil and with their heads shaven—once made dawn to dusk efforts to further the aims of Hitler's mad designs.

There is a strange sense of doom about this valley of grass and gorse bushes. Chunks of moss-covered granite lie under masses of tangled brambles. A gurgling stream bubbles darkly and runs swiftly down the valley where no one treads except those who make secret excursions in search of souvenirs.

And on top of the hill is an ancient church whose spire pierces the blue heaven, at which the workers must have looked so often and prayed for their deliverance from their hell on earth. Even the church tower was used as an observation post, a chamber was constructed in the spire and peep holes were cut through the lead coverings.

The only sign of a wound in the hillside today is a small scar on the north side, which was the original entrance. This was sealed up after the war when thousands of tons of material were removed and shipped to the United Kingdom as scrap.

Glinting and dripping with wetness, the main tunnel, most of which is lined, is like a huge curving section of the London Underground, with side branches leading to dead ends of rock faces.

The concrete roof is about one foot thick but here and there the naked rock shows through. From the arched ceiling of the lined sections, stalactites hang in yard-long "icicles" of calcium carbonate.

In one unlined section, which must have been abandoned when liberation came, trunks of pine trees at least fifteen inches thick were used as giant props to shore up the roof. Many of these have rotted away and fallen to the ground. Others are still pinned together with iron staples but are soggy, shaky and rotting away in the utter darkness of their tomb.

Before the authorities decided to block off the entrances, I made an excursion into these tunnels with John Hayes and Richard Heaume, two eager collectors of Nazi relics.

The ends of the tunnels in 'Hohlgang 12 Munition' are unfinished and are just as they were left by Organization Todt workers before liberation in May 1945.

German sketch plan showing two entrances in hillside which lead to tunnels below St Saviour's Church, Guernsey.

Christmas party of Organization Todt officers in an island hotel.

We had to climb over enormous quantities of rubbish and stumble and stagger around looking for a foothold among the rubbish which abounds and slosh through shallow pools of water accumulated over the years. In the flicker of torch beams our shadowy figures cast exaggerated images on these gloomy walls, but now and again the stabbing lights picked out dusty gas masks, steel ammunition boxes, an old field kitchen—its wooden wheels still in good condition—shell cases, leather pouches and thousands of steel helmets.

Some of the tunnel sides are bone dry and as we clambered over the six foot or more of old war material, it creaked below our feet. From the curved roof of the lined section, we could see the marks of the shuttering boards and the ever-dripping water falling around in sparkling droplets.

UNDERGROUND
HOSPITALS

As well as all the excavations made for bunkers, other enormous tunnels were blasted out of hillsides and the two which are now most well known were each fully equipped as hospitals and used after D-Day when German wounded were transferred to the islands.

At St Lawrence, Jersey, deep in the heart of the countryside, about two and a half years were spent on work which was far from completed in 1945. The estimated 272,000 cubic feet of rock excavated was used in the construction of other defence works. About 4,000 tons of concrete was used to line the galleries and walls.

The administrative section and waiting room for the "fortress doctor" of Guernsey Underground Hospital. Below is a 'Feldpost' box for letters.

Near one of the main entrances of the Guernsey Underground Hospital, the tunnels branch off into various sections.

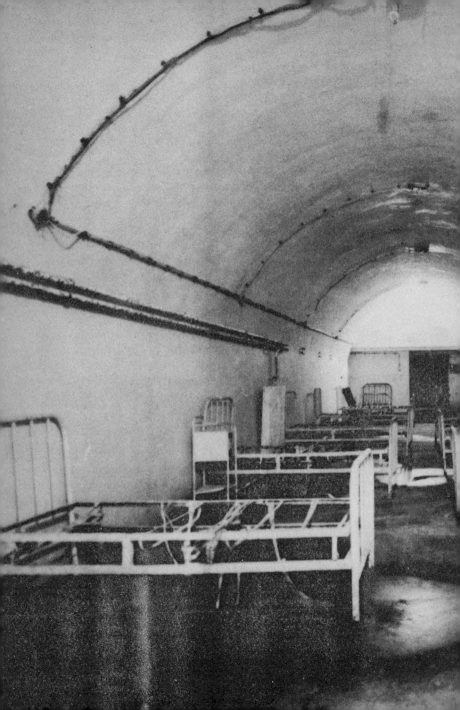

A ward with some of the original beds in the Guernsey Underground Hospital.

Two of the unfinished tunnels at the St Lawrence.

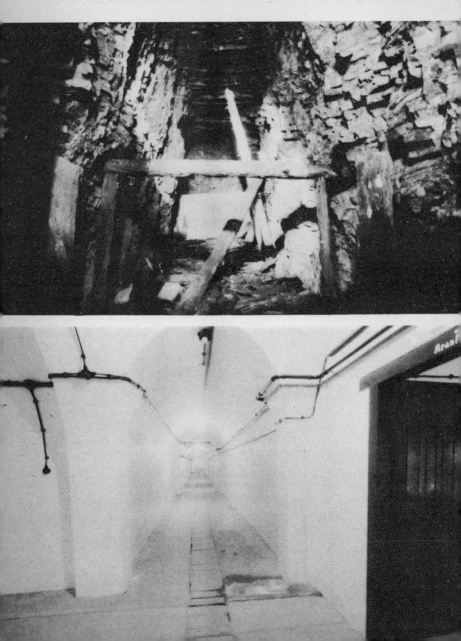

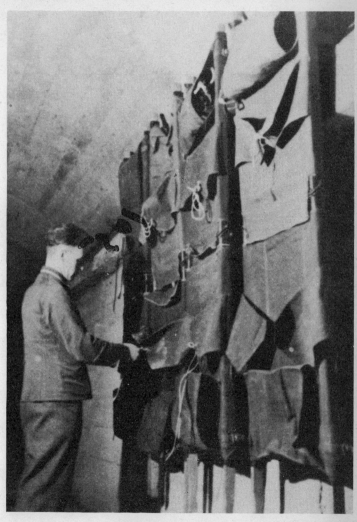

Stretchers ready for use in the Guernsey Underground Hospital.

In the heart of the Jersey Underground Hospital long corridors link the wards with the administrative part of the building.

The hospital wards were all fitted out and had emergency accommodation for five hundred patients. Soon after the Normandy landings, an operating theatre, a fully equipped dispensary, medical storerooms and doctors' and nurses' quarters were installed.

In Guernsey, the underground hospital was sited at La Vassalerie, St Andrew's, and some of the tunnels were designed for use as ammunition stores. This hospital covers an area of some 75,000 square feet. The wards are still to be seen where those wounded during the invasion of Normandy were tended. In each hospital there is an operating theatre, a kitchen, a dispensary, a cinema and a mortuary.

There are one-and-a-quarter miles of corridors in the Guernsey hospital and while the work was being carried out, seventeen workers died following an explosion and others were killed as the result of rock falls. Both hospitals were centrally heated, had air conditioning, hot and cold water, electric light and power and drainage systems. Escape shafts were also provided.

Entrance to the Underground Hospital, St Lawrence, Jersey.

THE LIFESAVERS

Operating an ambulance service during the Occupation was like conducting a private war for Reg Blanchford and his staunch band of men and women who worked hard and long at their Rohais, Guernsey, headquarters. Under Blanchford's incredible and inspiring leadership the St John Ambulance Brigade took part in a war of wits against the occupiers which no one realized and few appreciated. This five years' nightmare called for more than the usual amount of courage and resourcefulness and Blanchford and his men always came out on top, even to the extent of having private jokes at the Germans' expense and causing them embarrassment by making them run round in utter confusion. For instance, four RAF men landed in a rubber dinghy at Portinfer and were taken to hospital before the Germans knew anything about it.

Blanchford and his brigade were determined to do their duty to the island but they also found themselves in a position where they were forced by the *Wehrmacht* to use the ambulances to carry German victims of accidents as well as local people.

From the start Blanchford refused to allow the Germans to take over the service and he held the reins throughout, sometimes taking the gravest risks, when petrol was in short supply, by stealing it from German depots. When the supply continued to dwindle Blanchford was hard pressed to keep his vehicles on the roads and obtained an old furniture van which was converted by a coachbuilder into an ambulance. This petrol-driven vehicle was then converted so it could run on charcoal gas and was ready for service in September 1942.

This cut-down furniture van was transformed into a really efficient ambulance. It was operated with a little gasolene and a lot of good will.

This conversion from internal combustion to external quadruped was not so successful, but it could be made use of. The lamps, of course, were candle-lit.

When an injured 'Luftwaffe' pilot landed in Guernsey in his fighter-bomber he was taken to the Island's Victoria Hospital. Later, Blanchford and his ambulance crew, together with an armed escort, took the pilot to the airport on a stretcher, where he was transferred to an aircraft for conveyance to the Continent. While all eyes were on the pilot, Blanchford wrapped his camera in a duster, slid open the ambulance window and took this picture.

Preparing for the invasion of Guernsey this detachment blocked ambulance brigade headquarters and no amount of persuasion would move it. But so intent were they on the job of watching for the "enemy" no one saw Blanchford creep up behind a bush with his camera.

Troop movements to and fro past St John Ambulance headquarters were almost continuous. One day this troop was halted outside the station. While the two officers in charge had disappeared for a few minutes, a "German" mystery voice floated over the ambulance brigade loud-hailer ordering the men to come to attention. They obeyed!

After two further bleak occupation years, electricity was in short supply and it was forbidden to charge batteries by this means. Blanchford anticipated this and built his own windmill which was able to generate current and charge batteries. With further cuts in the petrol ration and a shortage of charcoal, the last resort was to obtain a couple of horses from a German transport officer and convert an ambulance to be horse drawn. The idea was good but after stripping the engine, gear box and back axle and fitting a turntable and shafts, the weird contraption was a dismal failure, mainly because of its weight.

But something had to be done and plans went ahead to build a horse-drawn ambulance which was accomplished by a local coach-builder from a hundred-year-old sketch and this was a complete success. After the war this ambulance was given to Sark and used there for many years.

With an old camera which Blanchford often took round with him he was able to snatch many unique pictures. He took grave chances by doing this and risked being sent to prison or even shot for spying. His pictures are incredibly good considering the conditions under which they were taken—through windows, from behind bushes, through the doors of ambulances, hiding the camera under a greatcoat and even covering the lens with a silk handkerchief.

RED CROSS TO THE RESCUE

"The Red Cross saved us." This is what islanders are still saying as many of them remember the grimmest days of the eleven-months' siege before the end came. As early as 1942 Guernsey's Controlling Committee decided something had to be done to get in touch with the International Red Cross headquarters at Geneva. The Guernsey Committee's President, John Leale, contacted Bailiff Coutanche of Jersey, who was some-what hesitant about the idea.

Coutanche and his advisers were afraid of the possibility that if regular supplies reached the islands through the agency of the Red Cross this might endanger the shaky supply service from France which local officials had done so much to start and maintain. It was thought that regular supplies from France were a better proposition rather than spasmodic supplies from the Red Cross.

Abortive attempts were again made in 1943 by the Guernsey authorities to contact the Red Cross. But when the sea links with the Continent were disrupted and finally severed after D-Day, 1944, the food situation deterio-rated rapidly and it became a matter of life and death. The islands were cut off from the world and the population faced starvation. While the Germans acknowledged that by International Law they were obliged to feed the population, they were preparing for a long siege. In August 1944, the German authorities said they had radioed a message to Geneva and were trying to get in touch with Berlin over the food supply position. They always took the credit for initiating Red Cross supplies.

Distribution of Red Cross parcels was made through grocers. Housewives with young children went with prams to transport them home.

The islands' authorities were then informed that the British Government had been told of the position and that the question of sending supplies was under consideration. Meanwhile the Germans decided that should Britain refuse to allow food ships in, they would wash their hands of all responsibility. They also made it clear that to maintain their own troops they would have to draw further on stocks of food in the islands.

At the beginning of November 1944, Bailiff Carey and Bailiff Coutanche were each

Every empty tin was precious. Island tinsmiths converted them into cooking utensils.

GERMANS HAVE REACHE

All Hors

Food: Mair

From

In outward appearance there garrisons and the Channe Famine and misery have redu Swedish relief ship Vega crept and civilians were more or l tattered and disreputable: the resemblance.

**ANNEL ISLANDERS AND
MON LEVEL OF MISERY**

Killed for
iet Cabbage

ERTSON

LISBON, Wednesday.

stinction between the German
s in the sixth winter of war.
to a common level. When the
ur they found soldiers, officers,
:—shoes, boots, uniforms torn.
low faces all bearing a curious
ie same

Vega is going into dry dock here,
but this is only a temporary

allowed to send messages to the Secretary
General of the International Red Cross at
Geneva, appealing for help. Confirmation of
the food situation in the islands had already
reached the outside world through the action
of a number of brave men from Jersey and
Guernsey. These men had escaped and had
taken with them up-to-date information on
the position given to them by certain island
officials.

**EVENING STANDARD: All horses killed for
food: Main diet, cabbage.**

SUBSTITUTES

The islanders became accustomed to the use of substitutes during the occupation. Here are some of them.

Tea . .	Parsnip, sugar beet, green pea pods, camellia leaves, black-berry leaves, lime blossoms, and carrots (shredded and baked).
Coffee . .	Parsnip, sugar beet, acorns, chicory, barley, wheat, beans, and lupin seeds (roasted and ground).
Tobacco .	Cherry leaves, sweet chestnut leaves, rose petals, sweet scented butterburr, coltsfoot, and clover.
Sultanas & Currants	Sugar beet, cut small and dried; elder-berries dried, and dried grapes.
Salt . .	Sea water.
Soap . .	The ration was increased by boiling ivy leaves till quite soft and adding one packet of soap powder and one tablet of soap.
Brooms & Brushes	Cane or rope to replace bristles. Stable brooms of wire bristles.

32

At the Hotel Metropole, Vice-Admiral Hüffmeier['s] headquarters in Jersey, a meeting took place befor[e] the 'Vega's' cargo was unloaded: Baron v[on] Aufsess; Colonel Iselin; Duret-Aubin (Attorney General) and Bailiff Coutanche.

Crates of Red Cross parcels being taken by trai[n] from the Guernsey docks to a guarded food stor[e]

During the first week of December, news came that a Red Cross ship was leaving Lisbon with 750 tons of food parcels. The Swedish vessel *Vega* finally reached Guernsey on 27 December. On that day Bailiff Coutanche left Jersey for Guernsey with Feldkommandant Baron von Aufsess, an aristocratic Bavarian known for his anti-Hitler feelings, to discuss the distribution of food parcels with Bailiff Carey. Also present was Colonel Islein of the Swiss Army and chief representative of the International Red Cross in Lisbon.

Vice-Admiral Hüffmeier, appointed in June 1944, to replace Count von Schemttow as Commander-in-Chief on 28 February 1945, put a fishing boat at Coutanche's disposal and after a seven-hour journey, arrived at St Peter Port. After the meeting at Grange Lodge Hotel, headquarters of the Guernsey Feldkommandantur, Hüffmeier—an ardent Nazi—arranged to have a fast patrol boat ready to take Coutanche home. This was the only time the Bailiff left Jersey during the Occupation.

After unloading Red Cross supplies in St Peter Port, the ship left for Jersey and arrived there on 30 December. At Hüffmeier's headquarters, the Hotel Metropole, another meeting was called to discuss storage and distribution arrangements in Jersey. The *Vega* made monthly trips to the islands and on her third voyage, she brought flour, stocks of which were completely exhausted and islanders had been without bread for three weeks.

The International Red Cross ship 'Vega' steaming out of St Helier harbour after her first visit.

LIBERATION

Jersey. It was liberation for the islanders and defeat
for the 'Wehrmacht' whose forces were quickly
rounded up as prisoners of war and taken to the
United Kingdom. Some prisoners were kept on the
island for a time to assist the Task Forces in
their job of mine clearing and other essential tasks.

Cartoon by Bert Hill.

On 8 May 1945, at 3 p.m., Churchill announced to the world, "Our dear Channel Islands will be freed today."

The war was over and the siege had ended. But the final surrender of the islands was not to take place without a show of arrogant defiance by Vice-Admiral Hüffmeier, the dedicated Nazi Commander-in-Chief who walked in fear of some of his officers.

Early in the month an Allied ship off Alderney had signalled surrender proposals which were rejected by Hüffmeier with the words, "You're wasting your time." On 6 May he made a dash to Jersey to organize a second audacious commando raid on Granville. This was cancelled at the last minute by Admiral Dönitz.

Next day the Union Jacks were already flying from some buildings in Jersey and Guernsey in anticipation. In the smaller island, to which Hüffmeier had returned, John Leale was told, "Put a stop to this provocative behaviour."

But on the morning of 8 May the Germans informed both islands' administrations that the war was officially over and that flags could be flown after Churchill's speech at 3 p.m.

In Jersey's Royal Square, where the white cross of surrender had been painted nearly five years before, amplifiers were put up and Churchill's speech relayed to a huge crowd. Bailiff Coutanche unfurled the Union Jack and the Stars and Stripes on twin flagstaffs of the States buildings and then spoke to the assembled islanders.

At that moment two British destroyers were crossing the English Channel. German soldiers were still armed and mingled with people in the streets. *HMS Bulldog* and *HMS Beagle* left Plymouth at ten o'clock and at two o'clock that afternoon were four miles off Guernsey. The German surrender ship, a dirty little minesweeper flying the swastika, stood by.

One of the happiest Liberation pictures ever taken shows Mrs Elsie Jory outside her home at Candie, St Peter Port. Her husband, Alan, anticipated the event by planting out 150 red and 150 white tulips the previous October which were in full bloom on Liberation day. Mr Jory also had the sign "Welcome at long last—LIBERTY" painted in his coachbuilder's workshop under the very noses of the Germans.

Captain Lieutenant Armin Zimmerman returning to his Commander-in-Chief in a rubber dinghy after refusing unconditional surrender.

Major-General Heine (right) shows his identification papers to an Intelligence Corps officer on boarding 'HMS Bulldog'.

On board was Captain Lieutenant Armin Zimmermann of the 46th Minesweeper Flotilla. In an attaché case he carried a paper authorizing him to receive armistice terms for Hüffmeier. Zimmermann · boarded *Bulldog* from a rubber dinghy rowed by three sailors and was met by Brigadier Arthur E. Snow, the chief British emissary who was in command of Task Force 135, Admiral Stuart and a representative of the RAF. The Brigadier said to the interpreter, "Make it quite clear to him (Zimmermann) that this is immediate surrender and not an armistice."

Zimmermann said he had no power to sign an unconditional surrender. He was given a copy of the surrender instrument with instructions that another rendezvous must be arranged. Before leaving he delivered Hüffmeier's last order, "The presence of Allied ships in these waters will be regarded as a provocative act." Zimmermann gave a Nazi salute and left. The *Bulldog* and *Beagle* withdrew for six hours, and back in Guernsey Hüffmeier conferred with his Fortress Commander, Major General Heine. At midnight an armed trawler left St Peter Port for another rendezvous with *Bulldog* and *Beagle*. A searchlight from the *Beagle* swept over the German vessel and a white, eight-oared cutter left the trawler. On board was Zimmermann with Major General Heine.

In the wardroom of *HMS Bulldog*, Heine was asked if he accepted unconditional surrender on behalf of his Commander-in-Chief. *"Ja,"* he said and signed his name eight times. In another letter, Hüffmeier stated he had already allowed the population to fly flags and hold church services. He maintained that there had been disturbances among his troops and this was the reason for his failing to be present in person to discuss the various points of the capitulation.

Ships of the Royal Navy outside St Peter Port after the Liberation.

Jersey is liberated and everyone came to St Helier to greet members of the Task Force. The scene at West Park where the traffic—mostly horse drawn— was still using the right-hand side of the road.

Brigadier-General A. E. Snow reading the proclamation from the steps of Elizabeth College, Guernsey.

Bailiff Coutanche had not spoken to his people for
five years. Immediately after Liberation he made a
speech from a window in the Royal Court overlooking Royal Square, "... I would ask you to
join me in offering thanks to Almighty God for the
deliverance of this dear island of ours."

Hüffmeier further stated that all his archives
and papers had been destroyed and suggested
that the disarmament of his soldiers should
not take effect until before daylight on 9 May
as, because of a fuel shortage, the fortress
billets were without light and this might
create difficulties. Lastly, he had no aircraft
at his command.

At precisely 7.14 a.m. on 9 May, when Heine
had finished signing, Brigadier Snow added
his signature and the Channel Islands were
free again. It was over seven hours after the
official end of the war in Europe.

At 7.45 a.m. Colonel E. G. Stoneman and
Colonel R. H. Power, with twenty men from
Task Force 135, landed at St Peter Port from
the German trawler flying the White Ensign.
News of the surrender was received in Jersey
soon after. *HMS Beagle* arrived off Elizabeth
Castle and an order was flashed to St Helier
for the Germans there to clear their ships from
the pier and to mark all vessels and guns with
white crosses and to lower all German flags.
It was Bailiff Coutanche's birthday and he
was taken out to the destroyer on board a
German pinnace, together with Attorney-
General Duret Aubin and Solicitor-General
C. S. Harrison. Three high-ranking German
officers, including General Wolfe, also went
out to sign the surrender documents.

Then a pinnace swept into St Helier with two
British Naval officers on board: Lieutenant
R. Milne and Surgeon Lieutenant Macdonald
and four Ordinary Seamen. They were the
first of the Task Force to land amid scenes of
wild enthusiasm and were carried shoulder
high to the harbour office.

**Brigadier-General A. E. Snow reading the procla-
mation in Jersey. On the platform with him is
Admiral Stuart and Colonel H. H. Power.**

Sonderausweis! Nr. Spezial 1.

Das Kfz. (Art. und Nr). Pkw. J. 118.

des A. M. Coutanche Esq.,

Anschrift Clos du Tours, St. Aubin,

darf waehrend einer Verkehrssperre benutzt werden. Seine Inanspruchnahme durch Dienststellen und Einheiten ist verboten.

Platzkommandantur 1 St. Helier 14 JUN 1944

Dienstsiegel

_____ Major.
(Unterschrift und Dienstgrad).

AUSWEIS. Nr. 334

Der Inhaber dieses Ausweises

Mr. A. M. Coutanche,

wohnhaft Clos des Tours, St. Aubin's,

Ident. Karte Nr. Bailiff der Insel Jersey

ist berechtigt, im Alarmfalle die Strasse zu und bei Kampfhandlungen mit einem gen allit. *betreten.* Strassensperren zu passieren,um nach St.Helier zu gelangen.

Jersey, den 15.7.44.

DER STANDORTKOMMANDANT.
Festung kommandant
Heine
Oberst.

The Bailiff of Jersey, Alexander Coutanche—now Lord Coutanche—holder of identity card Number One.

'Sonderausweis! Nr. Spezial 1'. On 14 June, 1944, this special permit was issued to Bailiff Coutanche to allow him to use his car when only about twenty private cars were left on the roads. A one gallon per week petrol ration did not go far and Coutanche's chauffeur used to push the car as far as the entrance gate of the Bailiff's home, Clos de Tour, St Aubin, and let it freewheel down the steep hill and along the road as far as possible.

In July 1944, when the Germans thought the islands might be attacked, the Bailiff of Jersey was asked to organize emergency accommodation at the Royal Court House, so he might be available at a moment's notice. He was issued with this 'Ausweis Nr. 334'—a special pass from the Festungskommandant to enable him to go to and fro from his home at St Aubin to St Helier, regardless of the military situation.

Aboard 'HMS Bulldog' during the first surrender conference. Left to right round the table: Admiral Stuart, Lieutenant-Colonel E. A. Stoneman, Major John Margeson, Colonel H. H. Power and Captain Lieutenant Armin Zimmerman.

The day British forces liberated Jersey. A scene near St Helier harbour.

Guernseymen greeting a sergeant of the Task Force which landed at St Peter Port.

German prisoners of war lining up on the sands between West Park and First Tower, Jersey, for embarkation in landing craft.

A liberation message from the King to Channel Islanders.

THE RAPE OF ALDERNEY

As the victorious German armies blitzed their way across France in June 1940, the nearest Channel Island in sight was Alderney, just eight miles away from the Cherbourg peninsula. It lay there like a deserted ship about to be scuttled, its evacuation having been decided upon almost unanimously at a mass open-air meeting after the demilitarization of all the islands.

The smell and sound of war grew nearer and the panicky islanders—with no more than they could each carry in a couple of suitcases —boarded ships of the Royal Navy and sailed away to Britain to leave their little piece of heaven which was later converted into the grimmest kind of fortress.

Between the time of Alderney's evacuation and its occupation a number of Guernsey people went to the island to save abandoned cattle and other property left behind. Guernsey's St John Ambulance chief, Reg Blanchford, was ordered to take a party there to remove the remaining dozen or so old people who had refused to evacuate. He returned with them to Guernsey on 28 June, the day St Peter Port was bombed.

The occupation of Guernsey and Jersey safely completed, the *Luftwaffe* dropped in on Alderney. This formal landing on 2 July was backed up by a German party which arrived by sea from Cherbourg. The rape of Alderney had started and it was not until 16 May 1945, that the German garrison there finally surrendered.

Much of what happened in the island during the war is still veiled in mystery. In the early days, working parties went there from

Target shooting. Fort Albert is in background.

A parade in Marais Square.

Guernsey, ostensibly to save evacuated islanders' goods and chattels. During 1941 and 1942, a permanent working party, employed by the Guernsey States was living in Alderney engaged in agriculture. Some workers also went to the island from Jersey. From May until August 1941, fifteen men of "Matthews' Sark Party"—engineers and divers who had been engaged in building a new harbour jetty in Sark—were sent to Alderney to maintain the Admiralty Breakwater. After their return to Guernsey no more maintenance was done to this important sea defence for Braye harbour and it fell into disrepair.

The agricultural operation came under Raymond Falla, a member of the eight-man States Controlling Committee who was also responsible for rounding up about 250 cows at the airport and having them shipped to Guernsey. Tractors, threshing machines and other equipment were taken to the island from Guernsey and the men lived in the empty hotels, cooking for themselves. Little contact was made with the main body of Germans and freedom of movement was restricted by the imposition of a curfew.

But it was possible, for instance, for a man to have a crab pot and to be able to dangle it off the end of the Admiralty Breakwater at Braye harbour in order to catch spider crabs. At Christmas, 1941, the Guernseymen held a party at their deserted hotel which was attended by German soldiers who allowed the islanders to celebrate under the Union Jack, which was strung across the room.

This strange twilight existence came to an end after the 1942 harvest. The men and their machines were shipped back to Guernsey and an impenetrable curtain of security descended. The Guernseymen brought back stories of forced labourers marching about with their Organization Todt guards. They saw all kinds of ships arriving at Braye harbour bringing cargoes of cement and guns and they watched the start of the building of many a blockhouse.

The **1941** and **1942** harvests were gathered by a group of States workers from Guernsey.

After the wheat was harvested that year, the Germans decided to tighten up on security and closed the island completely. All this time, however, a handful of people led strange lives there as servants of the *Wehrmacht*. Irishman Peter Doyle is one who is said to have been in Guernsey at the start of the war and to have gone to Alderney and stayed there throughout the occupation. He is described by one of his German masters as a "foreman and housekeeper". George Pope is another believed to have arrived in Alderney in a boat during the occupation and remained there acting as pilot and boatman throughout the war. With him were his wife and young family.

If German figures can be relied upon, the garrison in Alderney totalled 3,200 men at 1 September 1944. In addition, there were 40 Organization Todt officials. Included in the garrison were 1,150 members of the *Luftwaffe* and 590 German Navy personnel. Around the 11 miles of coastline, 30,317 mines had been laid and there was a very strong flat defensive system. There were three heavy batteries, one in constant readiness and two in reserve; 12 coastal defence guns and numerous searchlights.

Under a camouflage net a heavy naval gun is being installed at Fort Albert.

Peter Doyle, Sonderführer Herzog and Pilot George Pope. Doyle was "foreman, housekeeper and pilot".

Concert in the Royal Connaught Square. Left is the German Army headquarters, now the Royal Connaught Hotel.

Up to this date, two ships are recorded as being stranded and became a total loss. It would be surprising if there were not several others as these waters were particularly dangerous. Whenever a ship sank the German authorities were always anxious to attempt salvage.

In 1943 "Matthews' Sark Party" was forced to embark for Alderney from Guernsey in the steam tug *Alfreda*. A 600-ton trawler had sunk in Braye harbour and their task was to raise her. After striking a hard bargain with the Germans over pay, food and conditions, the party spent a week on the attempted salvage but failed to raise the vessel and returned to Guernsey.

Some light is shed on Alderney by Sonder-führer Herzog, a member of the Feld-kommandantur 515, the civil administration, whose headquarters was at Lloyds Bank, Victoria Street. Gazing through his horn-rimmed spectacles, Herzog wandered round with a black dog called Lux, a camera and a shrimping net. He took snapshots of troops on board ships, labour commandos building bunkers and installing artillery. Through his lens he recorded the comings and goings of his superiors and watched the progress of the Guernsey farm workers.

Herzog was finally posted to Jersey on 10 May 1942. In an album which he probably made up long afterwards, he noted a certain customs officer called Roseman who "in spite of the fact there was no work, was present with his subordinates". Roseman's presence in the island was resented by Herzog, who obviously took a liking to Alderney. He also noted that at Braye harbour "the small landing stage was less than sufficient for all the war material which was necessary to turn

The small landing stage at Braye harbour was all too inadequate for all the war material which was necessary to convert the island into a fortress. The sunken vessel is the 'Staffa', loaded with parsnips for Guernsey, which foundered after breaking away from her moorings.

the island into a fort", and took pictures
showing the harbour pier crowded with ships.
While in the island Herzog made a pictorial
record of a visit to Les Casquets lighthouse,
Der Leuchtturm Casquet, when a party of
Strength Through Joy went there. Les
Casquets, which comes under the jurisdiction
of Trinity House and whose keepers were
taken off in 1940, was garrisoned by seven
Germans, who in September 1942, were
captured by surprise and taken back to the
United Kingdom in a successful midnight raid
by the Royal Navy's Small-Scale Raiding
Force.

In August 1944, the battleship *HMS Rodney*
bombarded certain installations in Alderney
for two-and-a-half hours, scoring direct hits
on selected targets. Care was taken not to
shell the town of St Anne, though some
damage was done by blast.

Probably because of its isolation, the island
was selected as an outpost concentration
camp for so-called political prisoners. It was

the only camp of its kind ever to be set up on British soil and there, hundreds of prisoners are said to have ended their days, being starved or beaten to death by the SS guards. Other camps housed Organization Todt labourers who also lived under squalid conditions.

Although there were hundreds of graves in Alderney after its liberation, no positive evidence has ever come to light of the alleged atrocities and mass killings which are said to have occurred.

Lloyds Bank in Victoria Street, Alderney, was the island headquarters of Feldkommandantur 515, the German civilian administration with headquarters at Victoria College, Jersey and Grange Lodge, Guernsey. This party had come to Alderney for an inspection.

Outside the office of Feldkommandantur 515, Lloyds Bank, Victoria Street, Alderney.

A LA MEMOIRE
DES FRANCAIS
MORTS PENDANT
LA GUERRE
1939-1945

Visitors who go to Alderney today will see
two memorials to the labourers who died
there. One is a stone put up by French
patriots in memory of their compatriots and
the other is a marble tablet with the words
"In memory of all foreign labour who died in
Alderney between the years 1940-1945. They
also served." This was erected in 1966 at the
expense of Bert and Jack Hammond and their
sister "Babs" Tinson, who own the Campania
public house.

**Observation and fire control tower on the outskirts
of St Anne.**

**Stone erected by the French as monument to
hundreds of workers who died in labour camps in
Alderney. Another stone is dedicated to "all
foreign labour who died in Alderney between the
years 1940-1945".**

SARK STAYED
AT HOME

Sark braced herself bravely for the occupation which began as it was to end, with that indomitable matriarchal figure, La Dame de Sark, firmly in command.

Few Channel Islanders except Mrs Hathaway —now Dame Sibyl Hathaway—had the slightest notion of what to expect of the Germans, but right from the start she had them under control because of her fluent command of their own language.

From the moment Major Dr Albrecht Lanz, Guernsey's first Commandant and his chief of staff, Dr Maass, arrived at La Seigneurie on 3 July 1940, Mrs Hathaway commanded and received respect.

They honoured her unique position as leader of this tiny state with its own feudal laws and customs and next day a sergeant and ten men took over what appeared to be a token occupation.

Bob Hathaway, La Dame's American-born husband, stepped quietly into the background and Mrs Hathaway was mistress of every situation which demanded firmness, tact and an understanding which perhaps only a woman of this calibre could possess. She

Mrs Hathaway talking to three German officers who had called on her at La Seigneurie, where she remained throughout the occupation. When this picture was taken she weighed only 7 stone 2 lbs.

Mrs Hathaway at La Seigneurie with the British officers who arrived on 14 May 1945.

Mrs Hathaway with Dr Lanz, the Commandant, and the Seigneur, Mr R. W. Hathaway in the Clos du Milieu, a field adjacent to La Seigneurie.

performed a minor miracle in resisting attempts to erode her authority.

She sat firmly on her dignity and was respected by the highest German authority who cared to make the sometimes hazardous journey to Sark in order to be received by her. But for her insistence on staying at home and not fleeing in the face of invasion, she brought islanders together as never before and saved Sark from utter ruination.

If her decision had been total evacuation this would certainly have also meant the total destruction of Sark and all it has meant since it was colonized by the Jersey Seigneur, Helier de Carteret, four hundred years ago. As it was, each islander was free to choose and

La Coupée—the narrow road linking Big Sark with Little Sark—was in such a bad state of repair that the Royal Engineers, using German prisoner-of-war labour, reconstructed the complete road in concrete.

their choice was the same as La Dame's.

Resolutely, the Sark people remained on their farms and endured the slow deterioration in their standard of living and what remained of their freedom. The British commando raids, which were an excuse for the Germans to mine the cliffs, seal off the bays and send islanders to German internee camps, were blows which shattered everyone and caused bitterness and soured relations between the Sark people and the Germans.

During the whole period there were numerous problems which were incapable of being resolved but which were dealt with adroitly by Mrs Hathaway, whose people did not always see eye to eye with her.

Several bombs were dropped accidentally on Sark by British aircraft. These soldiers are examining splinters in a field.

During the early days of the occupation, German troops found Sark public houses well stocked with beer. Soldiers always removed belts and sidearms when on licensed premises.

Visitors to Sark in 1940 were few and far between and most were in field grey uniforms. Swastikas were painted on the entrance to the tunnel but nothing else had changed.

Two soldiers who were killed when clearing their own mines immediately after the occupation are buried in the cemetery near St Peter's Church.

But ultimately Sark came cleanly through and after an agonizing wait, the island was officially liberated on 10 May—twenty-four hours after Jersey and Guernsey—when three officers and twenty men of the British Task Force stepped ashore to find nearly three hundred Germans cowering in hiding and more frightened of La Dame than of any British soldier.

Mrs Hathaway's moment of triumph came when the first British landing party put her in command of the German troops until the main task force arrived.

Percy Brown, Sark's postman, delivering mail in the Avenue on August Bank Holiday 1940.

The war is over and it is good-bye to Sark for these German soldiers on their way to prisoner-of-war camps in England.

In Sark's St Peter's Church cemetery a memorial stands to a woman who meant much to many islanders. English-born Mrs Annie Rebenstorff had married a German and had lived in Germany before World War I. Mrs "Reb" made comforts for Sark children, sewed clothes, knitted garments and gave packets of food to deportees. She also obtained scarce drugs for sick people by bartering sugar beet syrup with the Germans. She died in 1958 and her ashes were scattered in Sark. Appropriately, her grave bears the words "The Mother of Sark".

IN LOVING MEMORY OF
ANNIE REBENSTORFF
"THE MOTHER OF SARK"
DIED 10·3·58   AGED 74

The harbour at Herm in springtime with a German
launch alongside.

Mr F. M. Dickson, who was caretaker in Herm.
The Germans called him Robinson Crusoe.

ROBINSON CRUSOE'S ISLAND

The former Crown possession of Herm, which at the time of the occupation was rented by Lord Perry, received little attention from the Germans. It was used as a training ground in 1940 and in 1942 a Flak troop was billeted there for about eleven weeks—during which time their only achievement was to shoot down one of their own aircraft!

During most of the occupation, Mr and Mrs F. M. Dickson remained on the island as caretakers. A commando raid was carried out by British forces in February 1943, at a time when no Germans were on the island and apart from agricultural parties from Guernsey, rabbiters and fishermen, the island remained quiet until near the end of the war. When von Schmettow, the Channel Islands Commander-in-Chief, was replaced by Vice-Admiral Hüffmeier, von Schmettow's chief-of-Staff was Baron von Helldorf. Hüffmeier must have suspected there was a plot against him so he banished von Helldorf to Herm where he remained until the end of the war. Von Aufsess was also deeply involved in what was, in fact, an assassination plot, but he was left unmolested.

Lord Perry—a snapshot of Herm's last Crown tenant, found on the island by Baron von Aufsess, a Feldcommandant.

For nearly five years Mr G. Macdonald and his wife were caretakers on Jethou. This picture—taken by Baron von Aufsess—shows Colonel Knackfuss of the Feldkommandantur with Macdonald standing outside the mansion house at Jethou. In the background is the islet of Crevichon.

For the last three-and-a-half years of the Occupation Baron von Aufsess was Feldkommandant. He was in charge of the civilian administration and travelled frequently between the islands. More interested in photography and writing and other cultural activities, von Aufsess was involved in a plot to kill the last Commander-in-Chief, Vice-Admiral Hüffmeier, which failed.

After the 20 July attempt to kill Hitler in 1944, Baroness von Aufsess was arrested in Austria by the Gestapo after she was reported to have remarked, "What a pity they didn't kill him (Hitler)." She was sent to prison in Linz.

Had it not been for the fact that the Channel Islands were besieged and communications were difficult and almost impossible towards the end, von Aufsess himself declares that his arrest was impending.

The Baron and his wife live at their ancestral home, Schloss Aufsess, in northern Bavaria.

When the Germans ordered the confiscation of all
wireless sets, a number of Sark people failed to
hand them in. One day a notice was found pinned
to this tree in the Avenue on which were the names
of all who were said to have kept radio sets. The
island's Commandant was informed of the facts
and said this was the work of a traitor, and completely ignored it. Ever since it has been known as
Traitor's Tree.